Name _____

What Am I?

> I am alive. I can grow.
> I make my own food.
> What am I? A plant!

Plants can be big or small. They can be smooth or prickly. They can be poisonous or good to eat. Plants grow where it is hot or cold. Plants grow where it is wet or dry. Plants grow all over the world.

Circle all the plants.

Color plants you can eat.

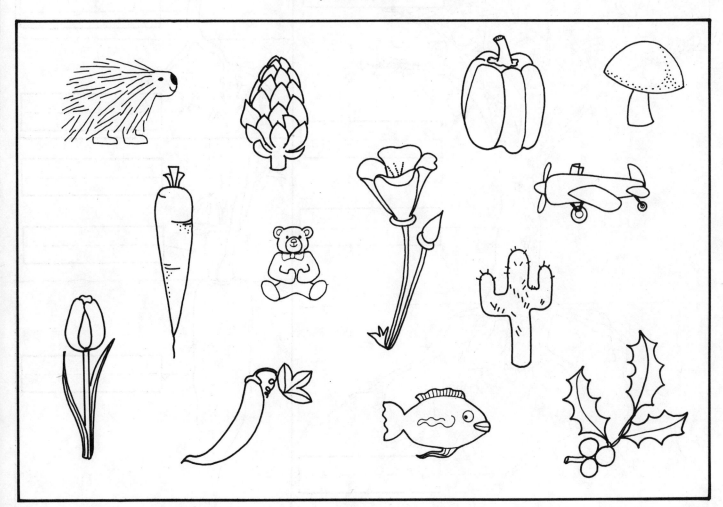

Extra: Draw a plant you like on the back of this paper.

Name _____

Name the parts of the plants.

| branch | flower | fruit | leaf | root | stem | trunk |

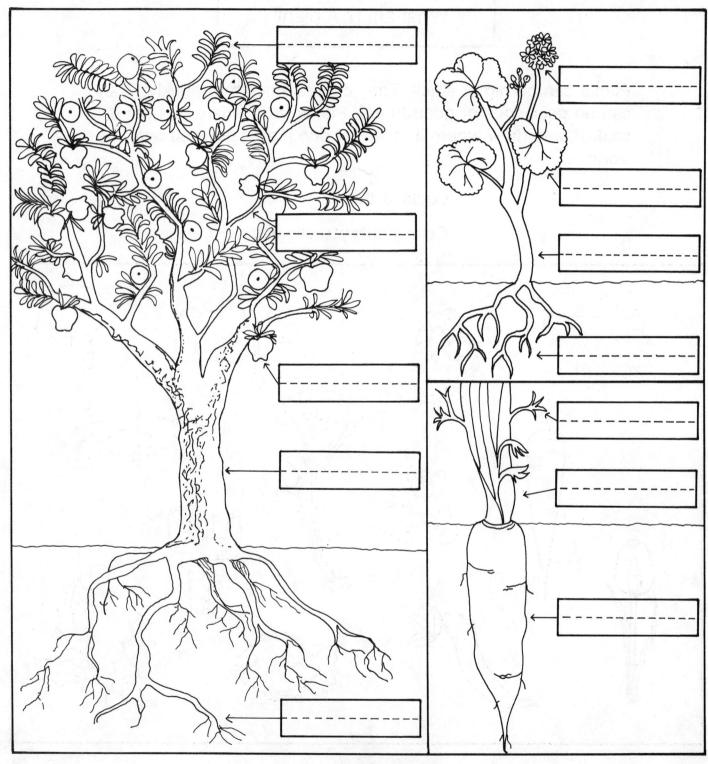

Extra: Color the plants.

Name_____

Roots

Roots hold a plant in place. Plants need water and minerals. (min-er-ulz). Roots take water and minerals from the soil. Roots take water and minerals up to the rest of the plant. Some plants store food in the roots. Carrots and beets are roots we eat.

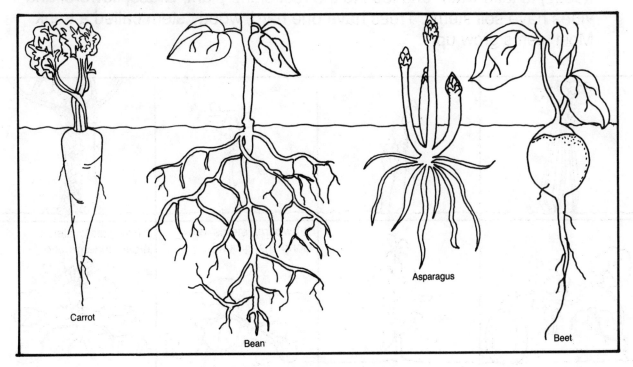

Carrot

Bean

Asparagus

Beet

Fill in the blanks:

1. Some plants store [_____] in the roots.

2. Roots take [_____] and [_____] from the soil to the plant.

3. Roots [_____] the plant in place.

4. [_____] are roots we eat.

carrots
food
hold
minerals
water

Extra: Draw a root that you eat.

PLANTS

Stems

Stems hold up the leaves and flowers of a plant. Stems have little tubes (toobz) to take water and food to the rest of the plant. Grass, flowers, and vines have soft stems. Trees have one hard, woody stem called a trunk. Most stems grow up.

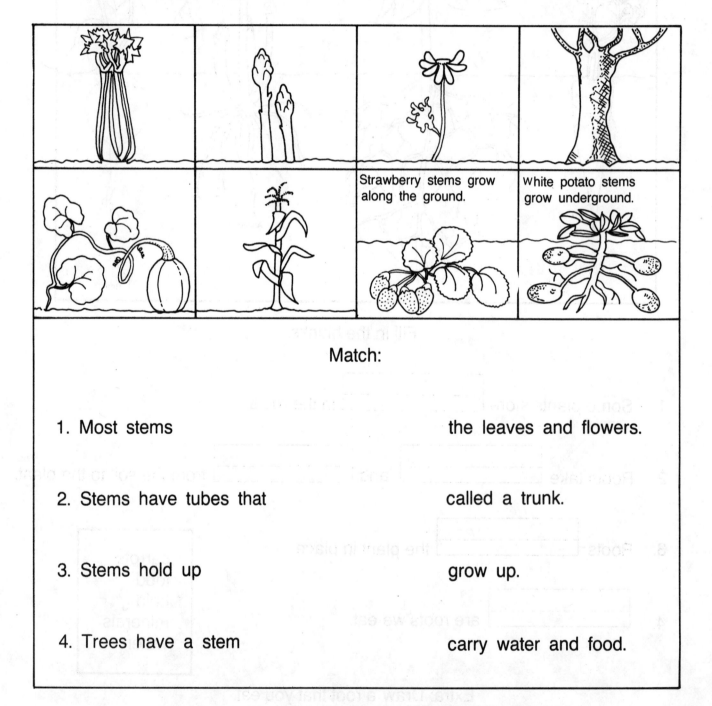

Strawberry stems grow along the ground.

White potato stems grow underground.

Match:

1. Most stems   the leaves and flowers.

2. Stems have tubes that   called a trunk.

3. Stems hold up   grow up.

4. Trees have a stem   carry water and food.

Extra: Make a plant with a trunk on the back of this paper.

EVAN-MOOR CORP., 1986

Name _____

Leaves

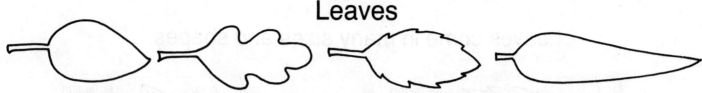

A plant can make its own food. The plant uses the green part of leaves, water from the soil, gas from the air, and sunlight to make the food.

We get food from plants. Plants make oxygen (ox-i-jin) for us to breathe.

What do plants use to make food?

1. _____

2. _____

3. _____

4. _____

Draw the part of the plant that can make food.

Extra: See how many kinds of leaves you can find.

Name_____

Leaves

Leaves come in many sizes and shapes.

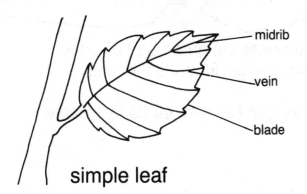

simple leaf

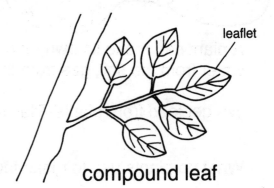

compound leaf

Color the leaves.   Match the leaf to its plant.   Circle the compound leaf.

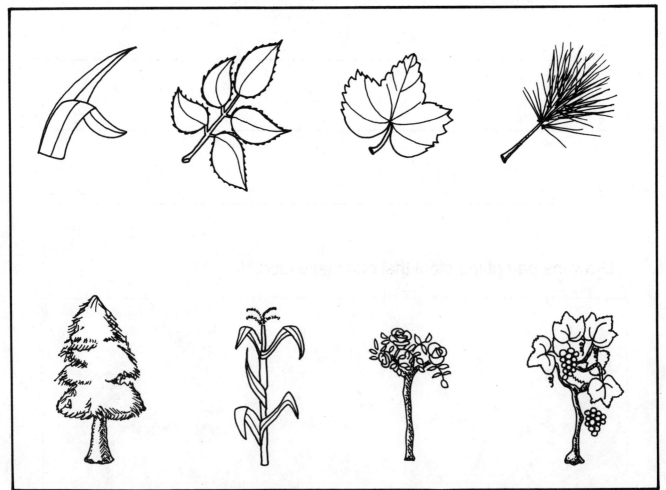

Extra: Leaf Rubbings
Find a leaf.
Put the leaf under a piece of paper.
Rub over the paper and leaf with a crayon.

Name _____

Flowers

Flowers are many sizes, colors, and shapes.

Tulip   Pansy   Morning Glory   Hibiscus   Daisy   Poppy

Flowers are not just pretty.
Flowers make the seeds for the plant.

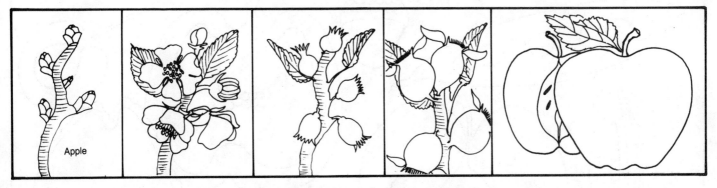

Apple

The seeds grow into new plants.

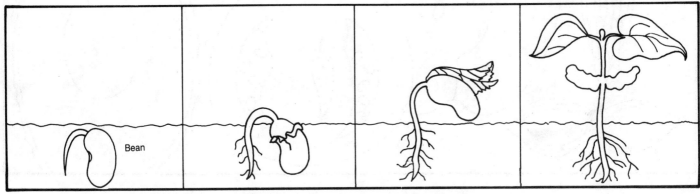

Bean

Extra: Draw your favorite flowers on the back of this page.

Teacher: You may wish to introduce these terms: germination, embryo.

Name _____

What is in a seed?

A baby plant is in the seed. The seed sprouts. A little plant starts to grow. The seed has food for the new plant until it grows leaves to make its own food.

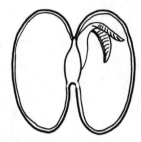

Can you find the baby plant? _____

Can you see a leaf? _____

Can you see a root? _____

Color the seeds:

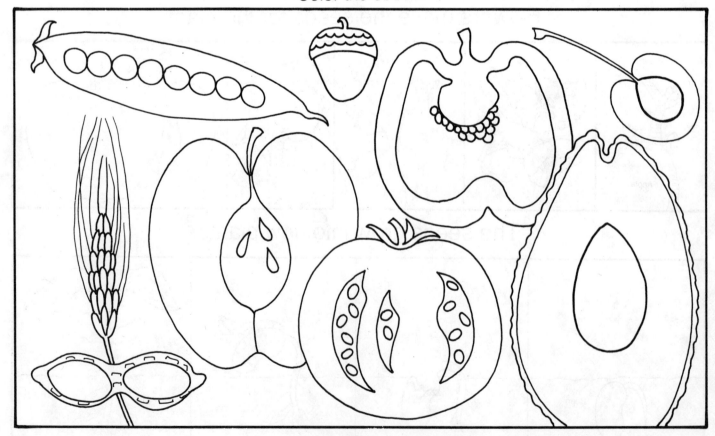

Extra: Make 4 seeds you eat.

Name _____

Seeds Travel

Some seeds move on the wind. These seeds have wing-like parts to catch the wind.

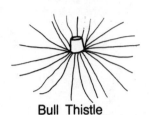
Bull Thistle

Ash Tree

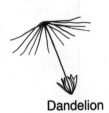
Dandelion

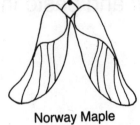
Norway Maple

Some seeds have hooks or stickers. These seeds catch the fur of animals. The seeds fall off later.

Burdock

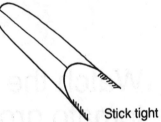
Stick tight

Queen Anne's Lace

Some seeds float on the water to a new place.

Water Lily

Coconut

People move seeds. They plant seeds in yards and gardens.

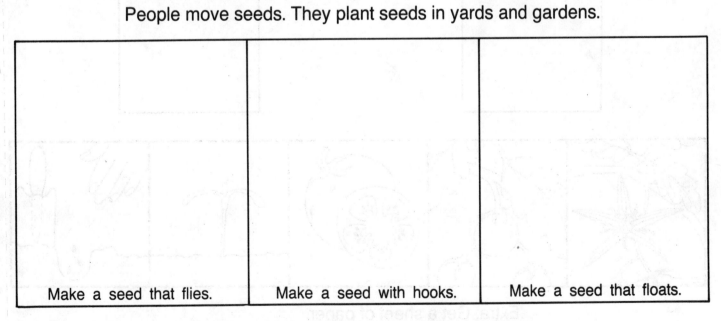

Make a seed that flies.	Make a seed with hooks.	Make a seed that floats.

Extra: Look in magazines for pictures of seeds.

Name_____

Life Cycle of a Seed Plant

Color.
Cut and paste in order.

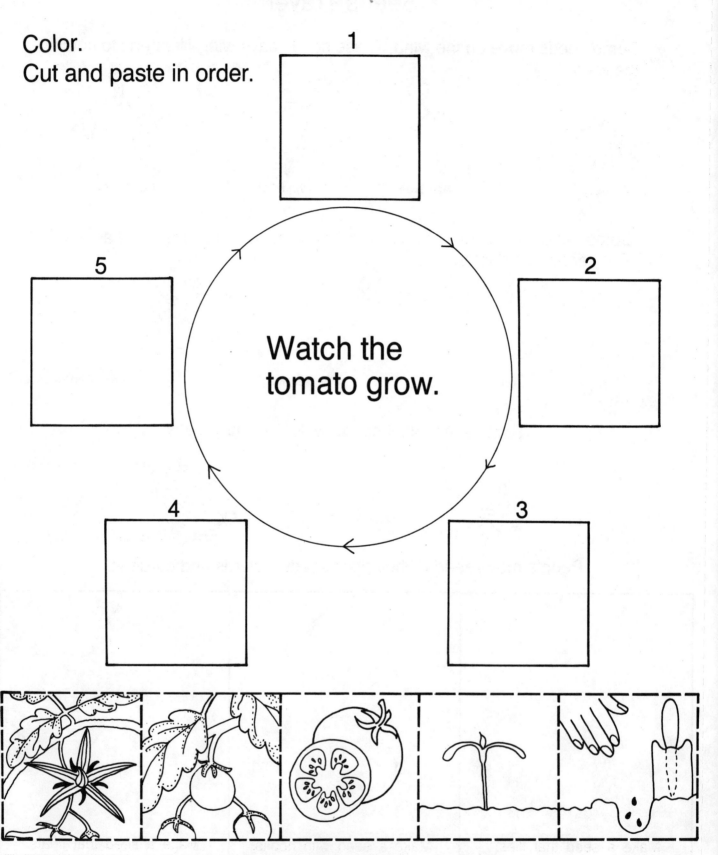

1

5

Watch the
tomato grow.

2

4

3

Extra: Get a sheet of paper.
Write a sentence about each picture.

PLANTS

Name _____

We eat many parts of plants.

fruit	leaf	flower
root	stem	seed

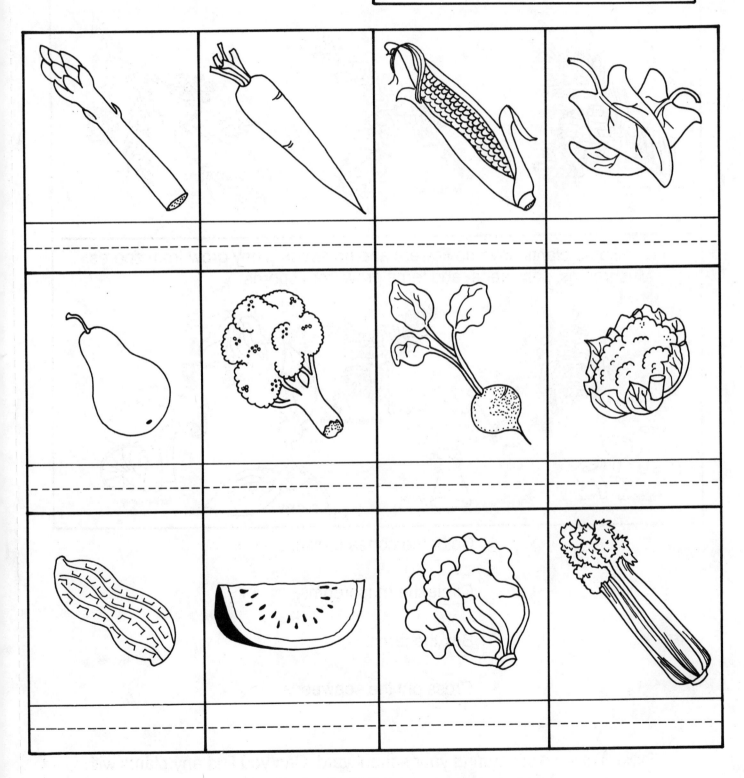

Extra: What can you eat that is made from wheat seeds? _____

Name _____

Plants With No Flowers

Some plants have no flowers but do grow from seeds. These plants have a cone to hold the seeds.

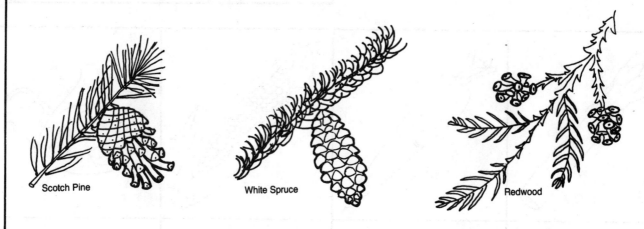

Some plants have no flowers and no seeds. They grow from spores. Mushrooms, seaweeds, and ferns grow from spores.

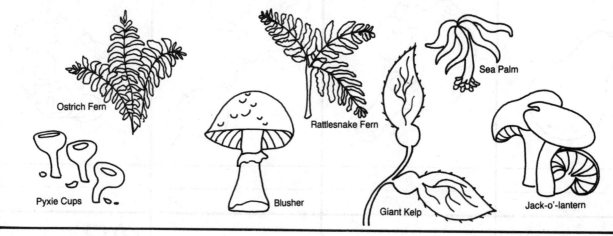

Color the cones brown.

Circle the mushrooms.

Box the ferns.

Cross out the seaweeds.

Extra: Take a walk around your school yard. Can you find any plants with cones? Can you find any mushrooms or ferns?

PLANTS

Name _____

What Do Plants Need To Grow?

Plants are like you. They need <u>food</u> and <u>water</u> to live. Plants need <u>sunlight</u> and <u>air</u> too.

1. Roots take me from the soil up into the plant. What am I? _____ _ _ _ _ _ _ _ _ _ _ _ _ _____	2. I am warm and bright. Plants get light from me. What am I? _____ _ _ _ _ _ _ _ _ _ _ _ _ _____
3. Green leaves make me for the plant. What am I? _____ _ _ _ _ _ _ _ _ _ _ _ _ _____	4. You cannot see me, but I am all around. Plants get the gas they need from me. What am I? _____ _ _ _ _ _ _ _ _ _ _ _ _ _____

Extra: Can you match these?

I need little water.

I grow in the salty water.

Name _____

How Can We Use Plants?

We need plants to eat, but plants are used in other ways:

lumber from trees
paper from trees
cloth from cotton plants
gum from tree sap
medicines from many plants
dyes from many plants

Match:

Look around the classroom.
Find something that comes from a plant.
Draw it here.

Extra: Think of a new use for a tree.

EVAN-MOOR CORP., 1986

PLANTS

Name _____

Plant Puzzles

Down

1.
2.
3.
4.
7.

Across

3.
5.
6.
8.

Word Box

seed	branch	leaf
stem	flower	plants
trunk	fruit	root

Can you find the same words here?

```
B  P  R  L  S  B  P
F  L  O  W  E  R  O
R  A  O  L  M  A  D
U  N  T  S  S  N  F
I  T  O  E  O  C  B
T  S  T  E  M  H  A
W  O  O  D  Y  S  R
T  R  U  N  K  O  K
```

Now find these new words: bark
                            pod
                            woody

Extra: Use these letters to make another name for flower.

loombss __ __ __ __ __ __ __

EVAN-MOOR CORP., 1986

15

PLANTS

This game can be played to review and reinforce information about plants.

Climb Jack's Beanstalk

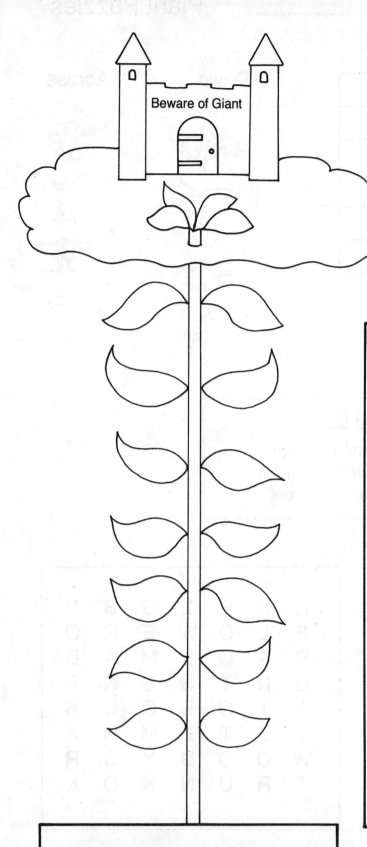

Beware of Giant

Place questions on 3 X 5 cards.
Put the cards in a box.
★Questions are more difficult. Child gets to move one leaf plus a free turn when answering ★ questions correctly.

Here are some questions to get you started:

Name 3 trees.
Name a stem we eat.
Name 2 red fruits.
★ Name a flower we eat.
What do roots do?
Name 4 parts of a plant.
★ What gas does a plant need to make food?
What part of the plant holds it in the ground?
★ What is the name of the green stuff in plants that can help make food?
What part of a plant makes seeds?
What do you call the stem of a tree?
Name 2 nuts we eat.
★ Name a drink that can come from part of a plant.
Name something in the classroom that came from a plant.
★ Name a plant you can wear.
Name 2 things a plant needs to grow.
What part of a plant makes food?
What are 2 ways seeds travel?
Name 4 flowers.

Make a beanstalk on your bulletin board. Each child will need a triangle of colored paper (Jack's hat) containing his/her name to use as a marker.